eMoviePoster.com

presents

Vintage Hollywood Posters VIII

Every item pictured in this book will be auctioned by **eMoviePoster.com** on the Internet from 12/08/04-12/18/04 (all items will close on 12/18 in the evening.CST; see our website for exact ending times). Complete detailed descriptions of every item (including high quality digital images and detailed condition descriptions) can be found on our website at
http://www.emovieposter.com

IN THIS AUCTION THERE ARE:
NO Buyer's Premiums
NO U.S. Shipping Charges
NO Sales Tax (except in Missouri)
See our website for full details!

IMPORTANT NOTICE:
In addition to the auction of the items in this volume, there will be a remarkable auction, Warner Bros. Movie Posters at Auction, from 12/09/04 to 12/19/04! Along with the items in this catalog, eMoviePoster.com will auction an amazing collection of over 2,500 movie posters, lobby cards and other movie paper items from a high percentage of all the movies the famed Warner Bros. movie studio ever made (from its beginnings in 1920 through to the present day)! This collection was assembled over assembled by a single individual over a 35 year period, but every item in it will be auctioned on December 19th, 2004. The auction runs from December 9th to December 19th (see our website for full details).

Edited and Published by Bruce Hershenson
P.O. Box 874, West Plains, MO 65775
Phone: **(417) 256-9616** Fax: **(417) 257-6948**
mail@emovieposter.com (e-mail)
http://**www.emovieposter.com** (website)

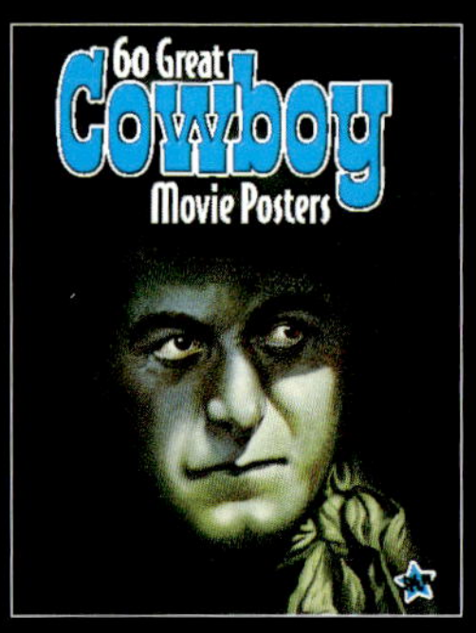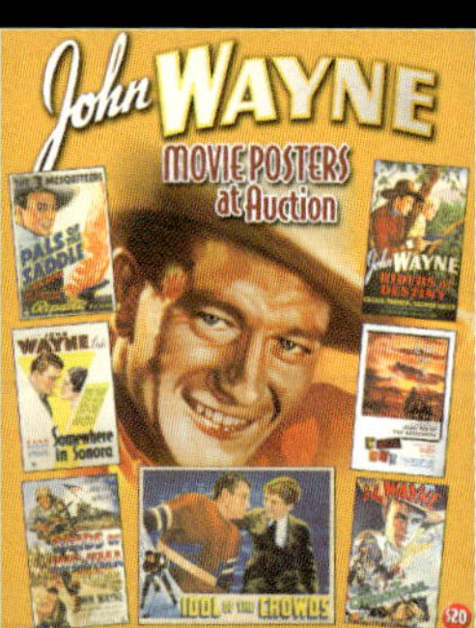

IF YOU ENJOYED THIS MOVIE POSTER BOOK, THEN YOU ARE SURE TO ENJOY THESE OTHER SIMILAR BRUCE HERSHENSON PUBLICATIONS. LOOK FOR THEM AT YOUR LOCAL BOOKSTORE OR ORDER THEM DIRECT FROM THE PUBLISHER.

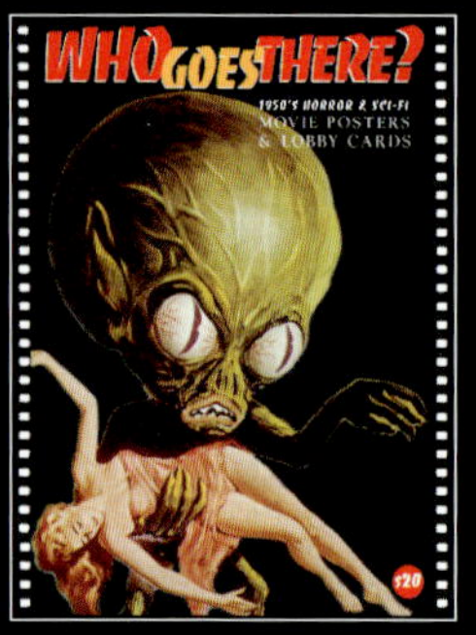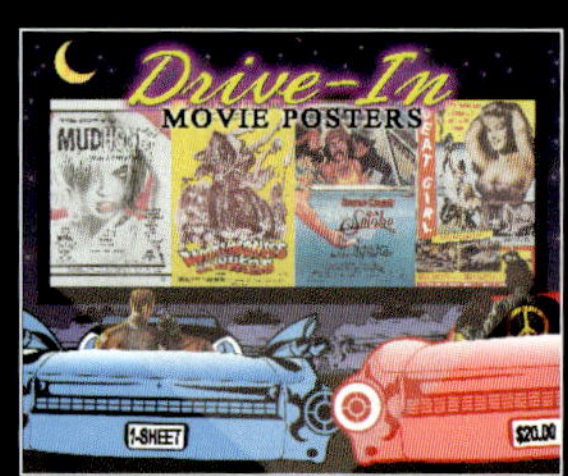

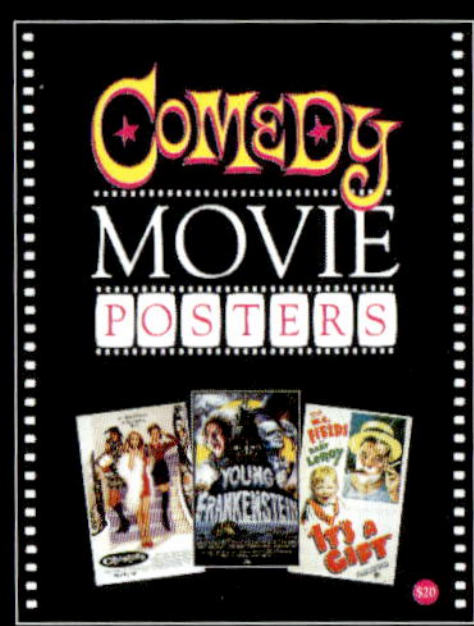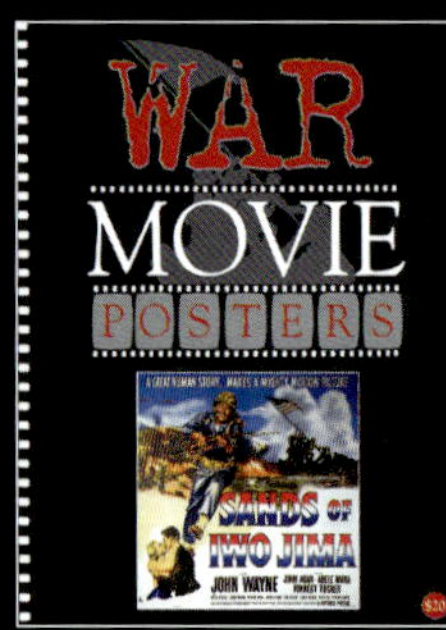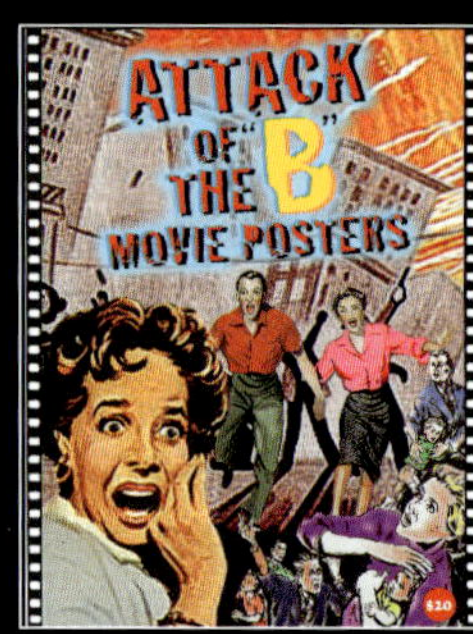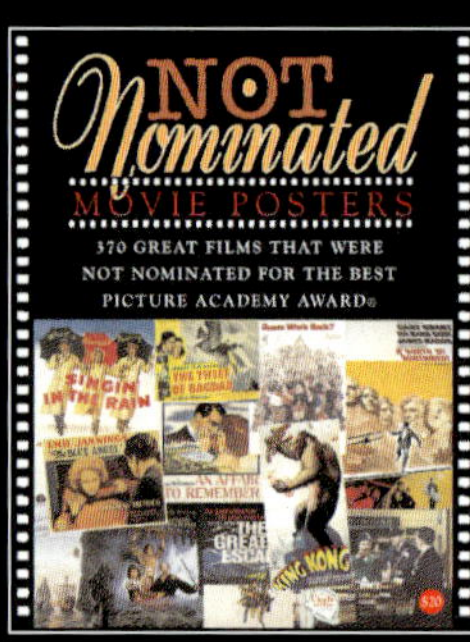

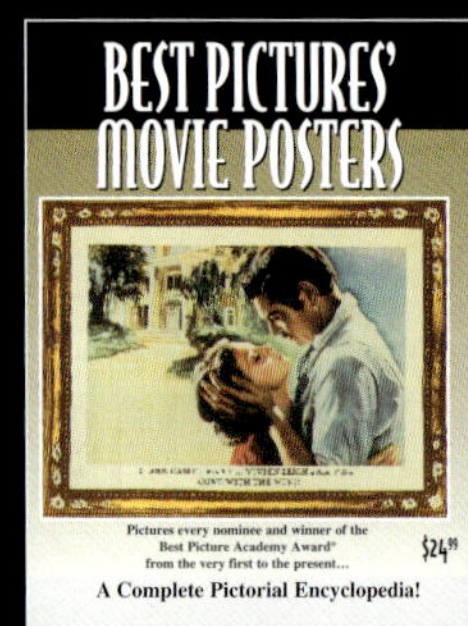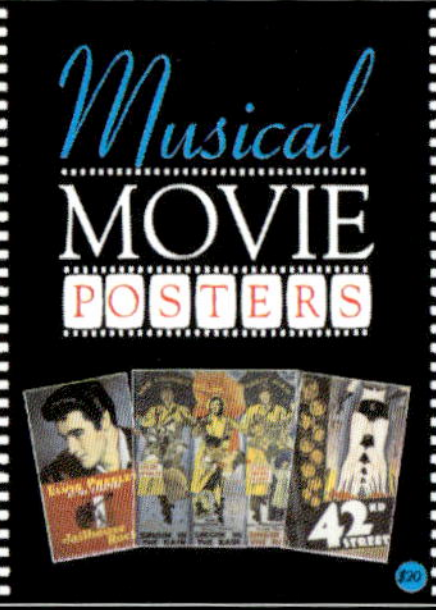

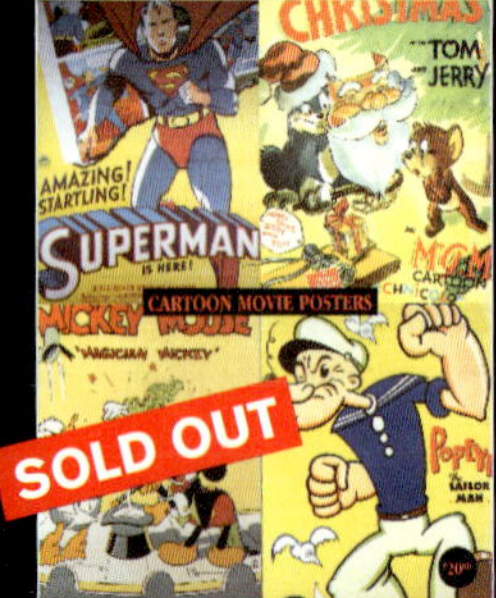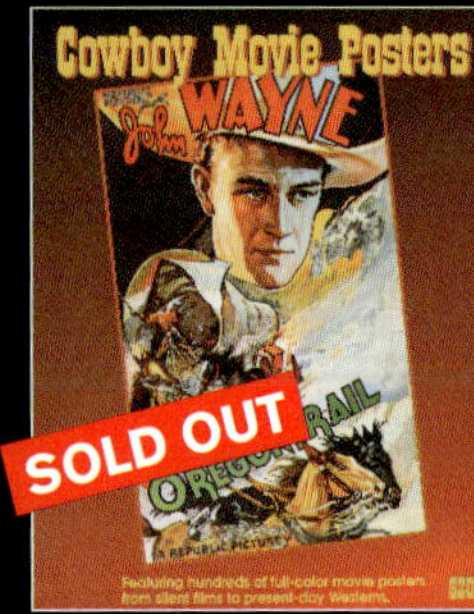

INTRODUCTION

My name is Bruce Hershenson and since 1990 I have sold over 23 MILLION dollars of vintage movie posters, much of it through public auctions. In 1990 I organized the very first all-movie poster auction ever held by a major auction house and since then I organized 12 more major "live" movie poster auctions (nine more for Christie,s auction house and three for Howard Lowery auctions) with total sales of just under ten million dollars. In between, I sold over 30,000 movie posters and lobby cards through semi-annual sales catalogs with sales of over five million dollars.

In 2001 I decided to move my major auctions to the Internet. On June 30 and July 1, 2001 (in Vintage Hollywood Posters IV), I auctioned 711 items for a total of $717,000. Those who have purchased items at other major auctions are all too familiar with the many added fees tacked on after the auction's close, including a buyer's premium that ranges from 15% to 20%, and shipping fees that range from high to outrageous. But in THIS auction, Vintage Hollywood Posters IV, there were NO Buyer's Premium, NO U.S. Shipping charges, and NO Sales Tax (except in Missouri). This saved most buyers from 30% to 40%!

I also provided complete detailed descriptions of every item. Many major auctions only provide bidders with fuzzy images (sometimes "enhanced", and sometimes not of the exact item being purchased) and fuzzier condition descriptions, glossing over condition defects and restoration. I provided high quality unretouched digital images of the actual items being sold, and detailed condition descriptions (including detailed descriptions of each restored item's PRE-restoration condition, something NO other major auction house provides). In 2002-2004 I have repeated the process with Vintage Hollywood Posters V-VII, with sales of over half a million dollars per auction!

NOW I PRESENT MY FIFTH MAJOR ONLINE AUCTION, VINTAGE HOLLYWOOD POSTERS VIII (which is being held in conjunction with a special auction of Warner Bros. movie paper (see below for further information). The Vintage Hollywood Posters VIII auction will end on 12/18/04 (there will be preliminary bidding from December 8-18).

ONCE AGAIN, THERE ARE NO BUYER'S PREMIUMS, NO U.S. SHIPPING CHARGES AND NO SALES TAX (except in Missouri), which will again save buyers 30% to 40%! Also, note that in Vintage Hollywood Posters VIII, you will find many items that are financially well within the reach of ANY collector. But I did not sacrifice quality to include these more reasonably priced items. I carefully sought out the most desired posters and lobby cards from the most collected films, the kind of items that most collectors are actively seeking, but have great difficulty finding, especially in top condition.

eMoviePoster.com will also hold another remarkable auction, WARNER BROS. MOVIE POSTERS AT AUCTION, from 12/09/04-12/19/04! Along with the items in this catalog, eMoviePoster.com will also auction an amazing collection of over 2,500 movie posters, lobby cards and other movie paper items from a high percentage of all the movies the famed Warner Bros. movie studio ever made (from its beginnings in 1920 through to the present day)! This collection was assembled over assembled by a single individual over a 35 year period, but every item in it will be auctioned on December 19th, 2004. NOTE THAT THERE IS ALSO A PRINTED CATALOG FOR THIS WARNER BROS. AUCTION, but that it only pictures 20% of all the items being auctioned on December 19th. The auction runs from December 9th to December 19th (see our website for full details).

AN IMPORTANT ANNOUNCEMENT REGARDING THE POSTERS AND LOBBY CARDS IN THIS VOLUME!

All of the items pictured in this book are the first release one-sheet poster (if it is a vertical image) or a first release scene lobby card (if it is a horizontal image) unless otherwise noted under the image. Note that we are selling many original complete rare sets of eight lobby cards, but that each of the eight cards in each set are being auctioned individually. All of the items pictured in this book will be auctioned by eMoviePoster.com on the Internet on 12/18/04. If you are reading this PRIOR to that date, go to http://www.emovieposter.com to find out how to bid (if you don't have Internet access, call 417 256 9616 and we'll make arrangements for you to bid another way). If you are reading this AFTER 12/18/04, you will find a sheet added to this volume that gives the prices every item sold for. If you have items you would like us to consider for our future auctions, go to http://www.emovieposter.com/consign.htm and read our terms, or, if you don't have Internet access, call us or mail us a list of your posters (see the first page of this book for full contact info). If you are interested in buying movie posters or lobby cards, or in learning more about the hobby, you should visit our website at http://www.emovieposter.com , where you will find thousands of images of the very best movie posters, as well as lots of information important to every collector.

You can find out all you need to know about bidding on items in this most exciting auction by going to my website, http://www.emovieposter.com where you can also view this entire catalog in an online digital format.

Phillip Wages (who created my online auctions and also much of my website) and Amy Knight (who did the layouts and cover design for this books and many of my previous books) gave considerable assistance in the preparation of this auction and this catalog, and I thank them very much. I dedicate this book to my children, Holden, Luke, Hayley, Samson, and Lucy, who gave me much needed support during the preparation of this auction!

Bruce Hershenson
December, 2004

1. THE GHOST OF FRANKENSTEIN, 1942, insert

2. FRANKENSTEIN MEETS THE WOLF MAN, 1943, insert

3. **THE HOUSE OF FRANKENSTEIN, 1944, insert**

4. **HOUSE OF DRACULA, 1945, insert**

**5. ABBOTT AND COSTELLO MEET FRANKENSTEIN,
1956 re-release, insert**

**6. BRIDE OF FRANKENSTEIN/SON OF FRANKENSTEIN,
c.1950s re-release, insert**

7-14. THE GHOST OF FRANKENSTEIN, 1942

15-22. FRANKENSTEIN MEETS THE WOLF MAN, 1943

23-30. THE HOUSE OF FRANKENSTEIN, 1944

31-38. HOUSE OF DRACULA, 1945

39-46. ABBOTT AND COSTELLO MEET FRANKENSTEIN, 1948

47-54. FRANKENSTEIN, 1951 re-release

55-62. BRIDE OF FRANKENSTEIN/SON OF FRANKENSTEIN, c.1950s re-release

63-70. FRANKENSTEIN MEETS THE WOLF MAN, 1949 re-release

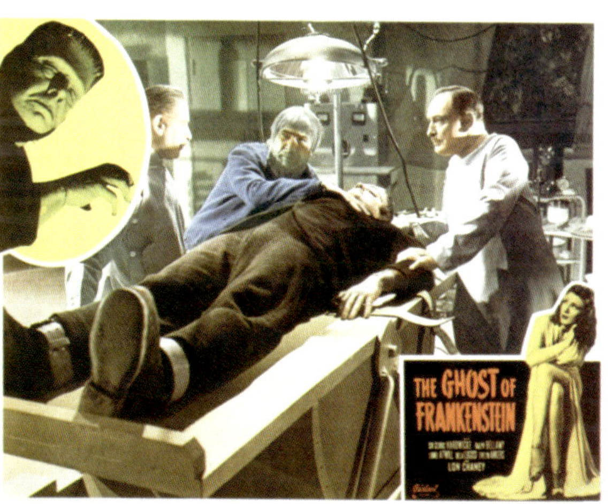

71-78. THE GHOST OF FRANKENSTEIN, c.1950s re-release

79. THE MUMMY'S HAND, 1940

80. THE MUMMY, 1951 re-release #3

81. THE MUMMY'S CURSE, 1951 re-release, title card

**82. THE MUMMY'S GHOST, c.1950s
re-release, title card**

**83. THE MUMMY'S TOMB, c.1940s
re-release #2**

84. DRACULA, 1951 re-release, title card

85. SON OF DRACULA, c.1940s re-release, title card

86. DRACULA'S DAUGHTER, 1949 re-release, title card

87. THE RAVEN, 1948 re-release, title card

88. THE INVISIBLE RAY, 1948 re-release, title card

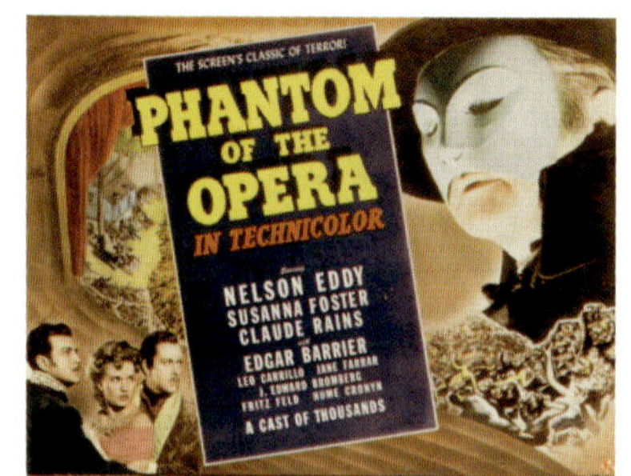

89. WHITE ZOMBIE, 1932, window card

90-97. PHANTOM OF THE OPERA, 1943

98-105. DR. TERROR'S HOUSE OF HORRORS, 1943

106. KING KONG, 1933, pressbook

107. THE SON OF KONG, 1933, pressbook

108. KING KONG, 1933, Grauman's Theater program

109. KING KONG, 1933, herald

110. CAT PEOPLE, 1942

111. THE CURSE OF THE CAT PEOPLE, 1944, insert

112. HOUSE OF DRACULA, 1945, Australian three-sheet

113. MIGHTY JOE YOUNG, 1949, title card

114. ONE MILLION BC, 1940, title card

115. THE APE, 1940, title card

116. I WALKED WITH A ZOMBIE, 1943, title card

117. THE LEOPARD MAN, 1943, title card

118. COBRA WOMAN, 1944

119. JUNGLE WOMAN, 1944, title card

120. JUNGLE CAPTIVE, 1945, title card

121. THE UNDYING MONSTER, 1942, title card

122. THE LODGER, 1943, title card

123. REVENGE OF THE ZOMBIES, 1943, title card

124. REVENGE OF THE ZOMBIES, 1943

125. THE INVISIBLE MAN'S REVENGE, 1944, title card

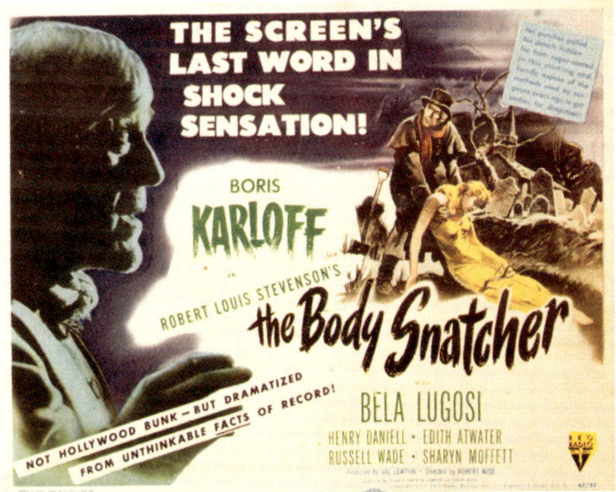

126. THE BODY SNATCHER, 1945, title card

127. BEDLAM, 1946, title card

128. HOUSE OF HORRORS, 1946, title card

130. THE TRAIL OF THE OCTOPUS, 1919

131. PEACEFUL VALLEY, 1920

132. PETER THE TRAMP, 1922, Swedish

129. MY FRIEND THE DEVIL, 1922, three-sheet

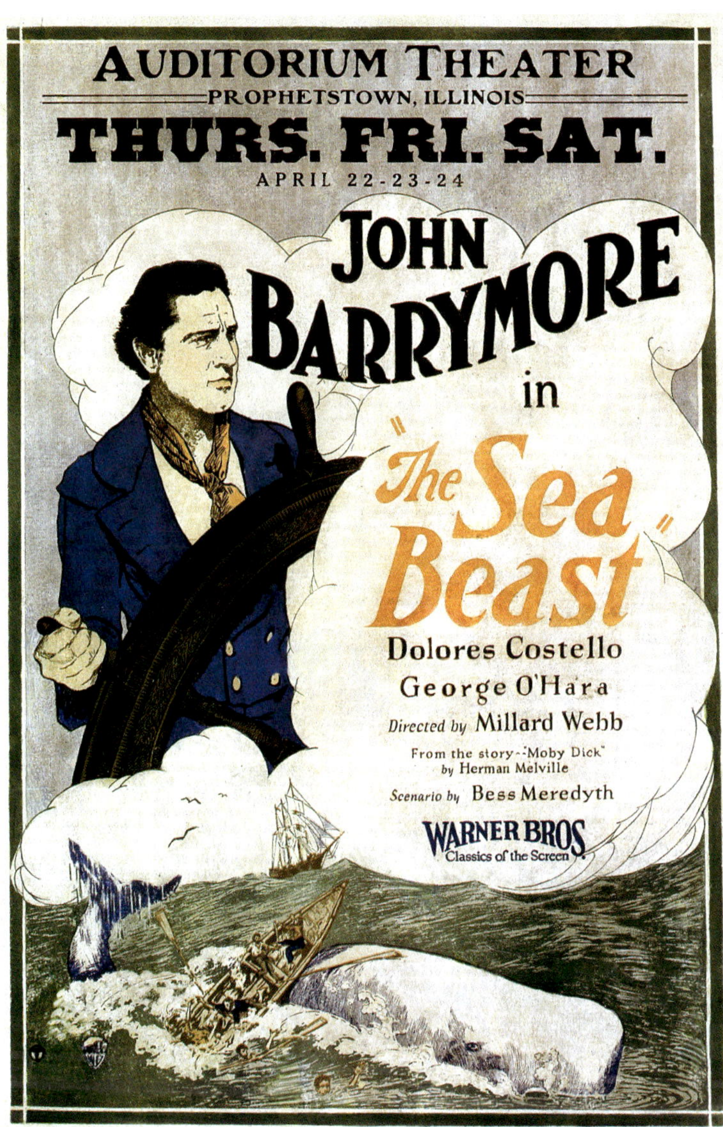

133. THE SEA BEAST, 1926, window card

134. FREE & EASY, 1930

135. MONSIEUR BEAUCAIRE, 1924, Swedish

136. THE ENEMY, 1927, Swedish

137. CHEYENNE, 1929

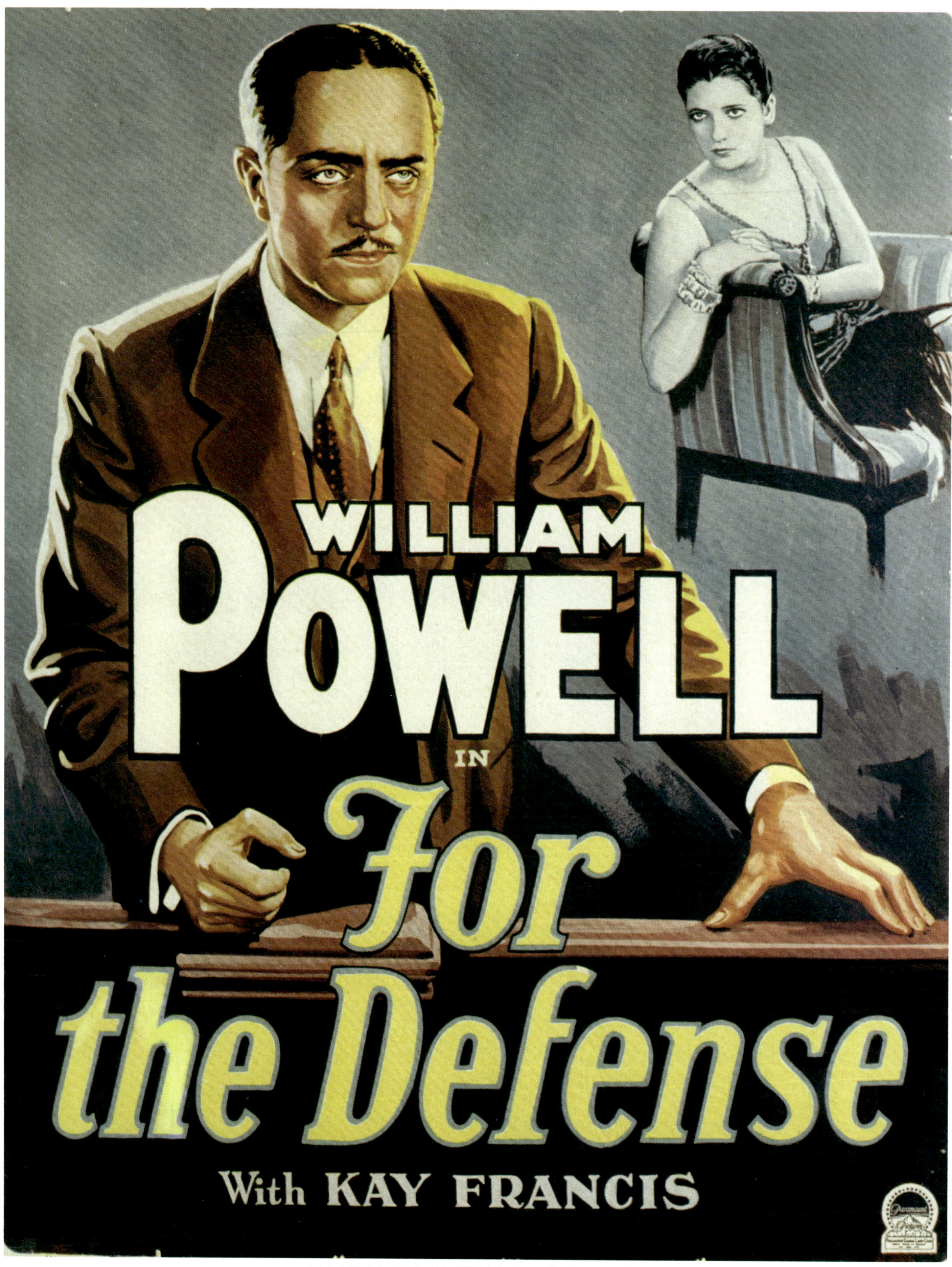

138. FOR THE DEFENSE, 1930, window card

139. ALL QUIET ON THE WESTERN FRONT, 1930

140. AROUND THE WORLD WITH BURTON HOLMES, 1930

141. TODAY WE LIVE, 1933

142. THE SONG OF SONGS, 1933, jumbo lobby card

143. MUTINY ON THE BOUNTY, 1935

144. DEAD END, 1937

145. WINNER TAKE ALL, 1932, window card

146. HARD TO HANDLE, 1933, title card

147. RED DUST, 1932

148. TOP HAT, 1935, half-sheet

149. THE WIZARD OF OZ, 1939

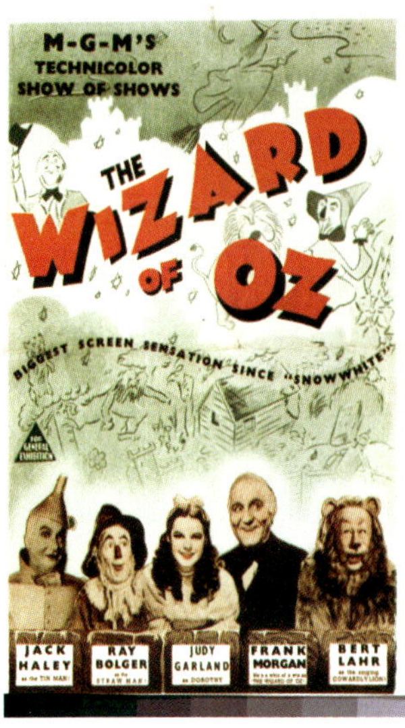

150. THE WIZARD OF OZ, 1939, Australian herald

151. SNOW WHITE & THE SEVEN DWARFS, 1938, Australian herald

152. A NIGHT AT THE OPERA, 1935, Australian herald

153. A DAY AT THE RACES, 1937, Australian herald

154. THE BRIDE OF FRANKENSTEIN, 1935, Australian herald

155. SON OF FRANKENSTEIN, 1939, Australian herald

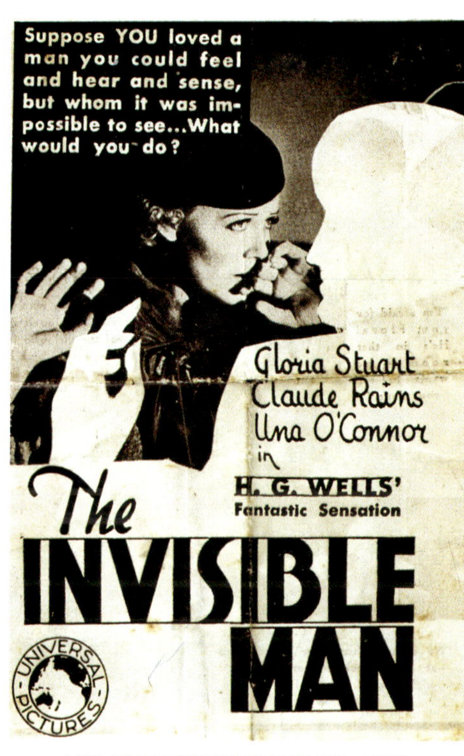

156. THE INVISIBLE MAN, 1933, Australian herald

157. FLASH GORDON, 1936, Australian herald

158. BUCK ROGERS, 1940, Australian herald

159. FLYING DOWN TO RIO, 1933, Australian herald

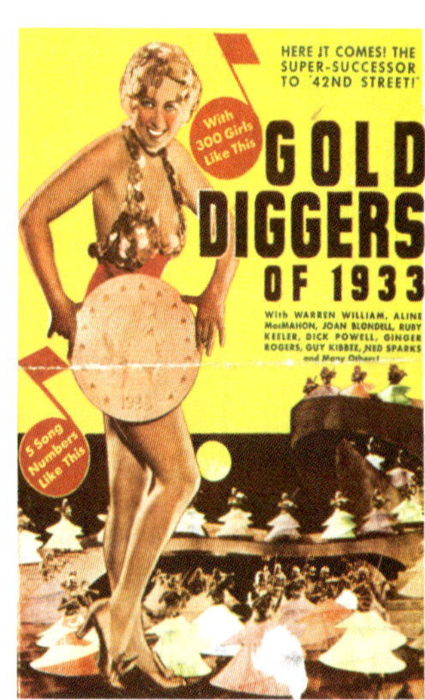

160. GOLD DIGGERS OF 1933, 1933, Australian herald

161-168. FLASH GORDON, 1936

169. PACK UP YOUR TROUBLES, 1932

170. DUCK SOUP, 1933, window card

171. MODERN TIMES, 1936, Czech

172. A NIGHT IN CASABLANCA, 1946, title card

173. MICRO-PHONIES, 1945, title card

174. MILLION DOLLAR LEGS, 1932

175. IF I HAD A MILLION, 1932

176. THE BARBER SHOP, 1933

177. TILLIE & GUS, 1933

178. INTERNATIONAL HOUSE, 1933

179. YOU'RE TELLING ME, 1934

180. IT'S A GIFT, 1934

181. THE OLD-FASHIONED WAY, 1934

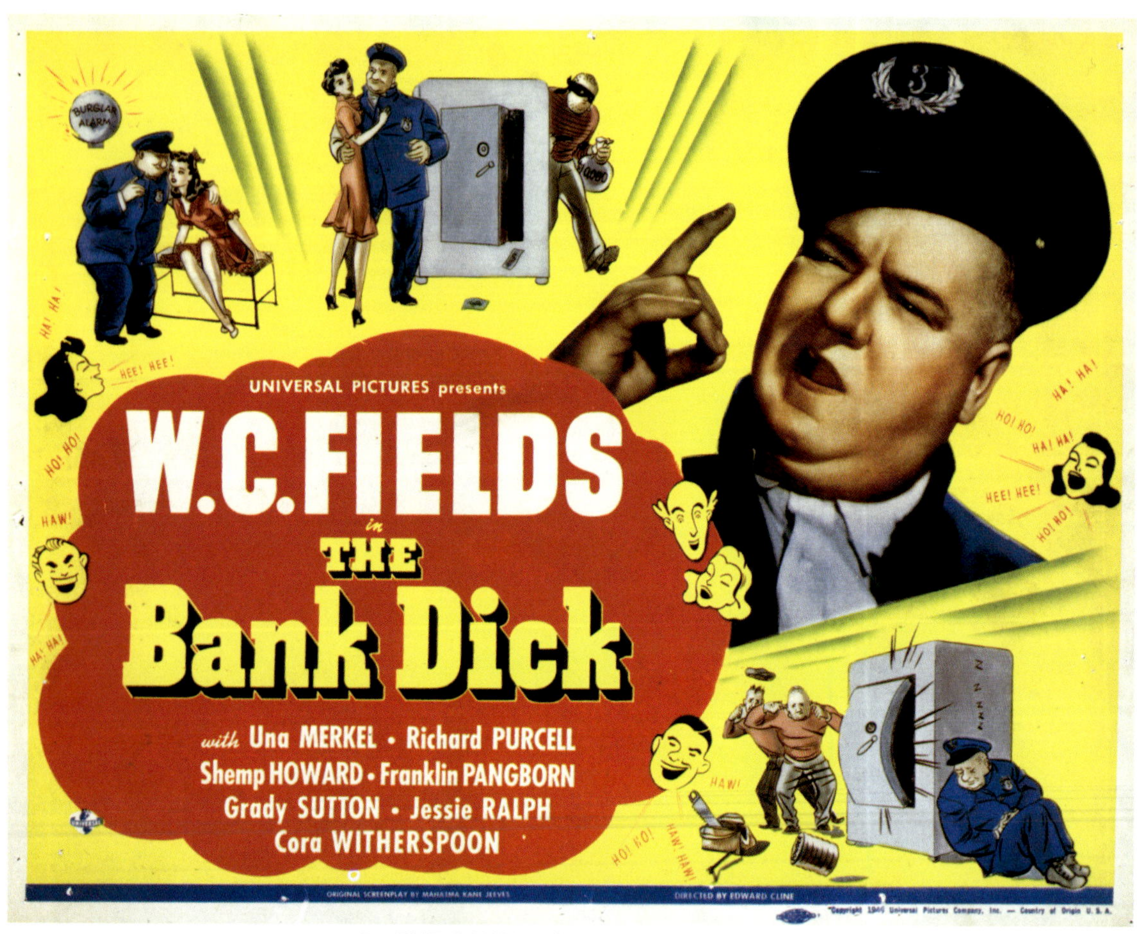

182. THE BANK DICK, 1940, title card

183. MRS WIGGS OF THE CABBAGE PATCH, 1934

184. DAVID COPPERFIELD, 1935

185. MAN ON THE FLYING TRAPEZE, 1935

186. MISSISSIPPI, 1935

187. POPPY, 1936

188. THE BIG BROADCAST OF 1938, 1938

189. YOU CAN'T CHEAT AN HONEST MAN, 1939

190. MY LITTLE CHICKADEE, 1940

191. NEVER GIVE A SUCKER AN EVEN BREAK, 1941, title card

192. NEVER GIVE A SUCKER AN EVEN BREAK, 1941

193. NEVER GIVE A SUCKER AN EVEN BREAK, 1941

194. FOLLOW THE BOYS, 1944

195. SONG OF THE OPEN ROAD, 1944

196. SENSATIONS OF 1945, 1944

197. FLYING DOWN TO RIO, c.1940s, first Belgian release

198. CAMILLE, c.1950s, first Japanese release

199. THE WIZARD OF OZ, 1949 re-release

200. ONE MILLION B.C., 1940, insert

201. JUNGLE BOOK, 1942, insert

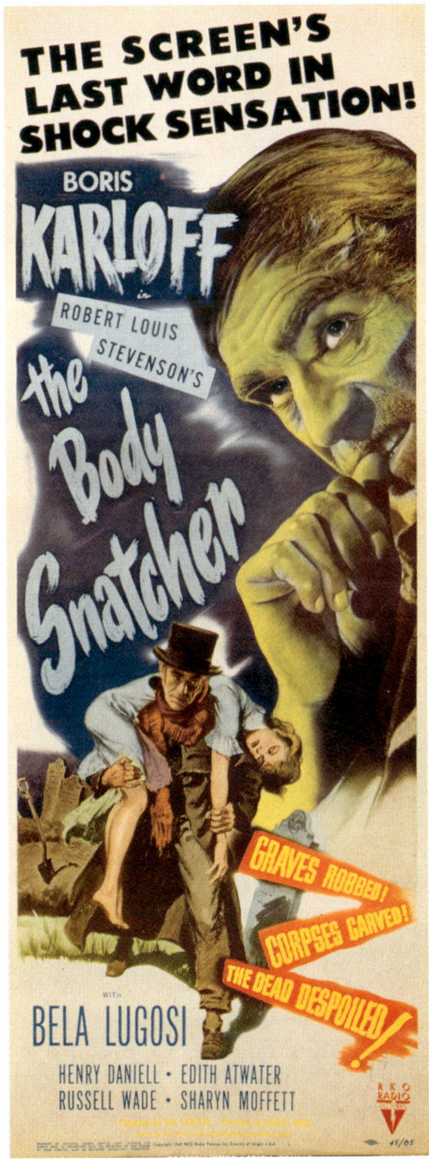

202. THE BODY SNATCHER, 1945, insert

203. THE MARK OF ZORRO, 1940

204. CITIZEN KANE, 1940

205. THE LADY VANISHES, 1938

206. THIS GUN FOR HIRE, 1942

207. THIS GUN FOR HIRE, 1942

208. THE THIN MAN, 1934

209. MANHATTAN MELODRAMA, 1934

**210. YOUNG & INNOCENT, 1937,
(also released as THE GIRL WAS YOUNG)**

211. NOTORIOUS, 1946, set of 4 'key' door hangers

212. LAURA, 1944, three-sheet

213. REAR WINDOW, 1954, insert

214. VERTIGO, 1958, insert

215. NOTORIOUS, 1946, half-sheet

216. THE 39 STEPS, 1938 re-release

217. MURDER MY SWEET, 1944, Australian daybill

218. VERTIGO, 1958 #6

219. REAR WINDOW, 1954, Belgian

220. MYSTERIOUS MR. MOTO, 1938

221. MR. MOTO'S LAST WARNING, 1939

222. MR. MOTO'S GAMBLE, 1938, title card

223. MR. MOTO'S GAMBLE, 1938

224. SHERLOCK HOLMES IN WASHINGTON, 1942

225. SHERLOCK HOLMES AND THE VOICE OF TERROR, 1942

226. SHERLOCK HOLMES FACES DEATH, 1943

227. THE SCARLET CLAW, 1944

228. THE SCARLET CLAW, 1944

229. THE SCARLET CLAW, 1944

230. THE HOUSE OF FEAR, 1944, title card

231. SHERLOCK HOLMES & THE SPIDER WOMAN, 1944

232. SHERLOCK HOLMES & THE SPIDER WOMAN, 1944

233. THE PEARL OF DEATH, 1944, title card

234. THE WOMAN IN GREEN, 1945, title card

235. PURSUIT TO ALGIERS, 1945

236. DRESSED TO KILL, 1946

237. TERROR BY NIGHT, 1946

238. DICK TRACY, 1945, title card

239. DICK TRACY, 1945

240. DICK TRACY VS. CUEBALL, 1946, title card

241. DICK TRACY VS. CUEBALL, 1946 #2

242. DICK TRACY MEETS GRUESOME, 1947, title card

243. DICK TRACY MEETS GRUESOME, 1947 #2

244. DICK TRACY'S DILEMMA, 1947, title card

245. DICK TRACY'S DILEMMA, 1947 #3

246. BICYCLE THIEF, 1948, 12 Italian photobustas

247. BICYCLE THIEF, 1948, Italian locandina

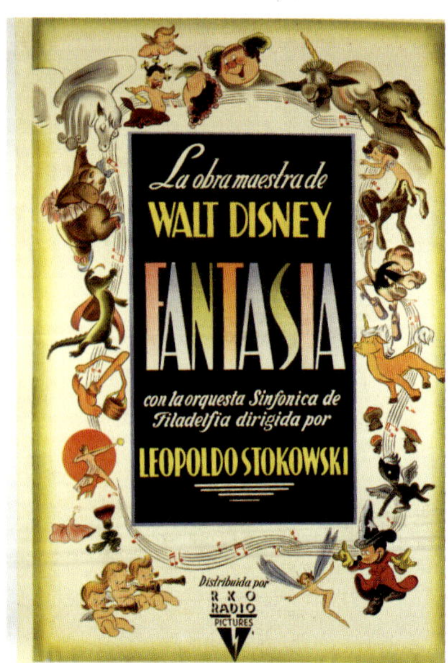

248. FANTASIA, 1941, Argentinean

249. ZIEGFELD FOLLIES, 1945, title card

250. CITIZEN KANE, 1948 re-release,
Italian one-panel

251. IT'S A WONDERFUL LIFE, 1946

252. MACBETH, 1948

253. THE 7TH VICTIM, 1944, title card

254. MRS MINIVER, 1960,
first German release

255. RED RIVER, 1948, Belgian

256. THE PICTURE OF DORIAN GRAY, 1945,
title card

257. THE GHOST SHIP, 1943

258. THE THIEF OF BAGDAD, 1940

259-266. THE THIEF OF BAGDAD, 1940

267. SWEET SMELL OF SUCCESS, 1957

268. THE MONSTER THAT CHALLENGED THE WORLD, 1957, Italian one-panel

269. CURSE OF THE UNDEAD, 1959

270. SANDS OF IWO JIMA, 1950, Japanese two panel

271. HARVEY, 1950, insert

272. THE NIGHT OF THE HUNTER, 1955 #3

273. HARVEY, 1950 #4

274. THE SEVEN YEAR ITCH, 1955, half-sheet

275. THE SEVEN YEAR ITCH, 1955, Belgian

276. THE DAY THE EARTH STOOD STILL, 1951

277. REVENGE OF THE CREATURE, 1955, three-sheet

278. FORBIDDEN PLANET, 1956

279. FORBIDDEN PLANET, 1956, insert

280. FORBIDDEN PLANET, 1956, Australian daybill

281. REVENGE OF THE CREATURE, 1955, insert

282. REVENGE OF THE CREATURE, 1955, Australian daybill

283. FORBIDDEN PLANET, 1956, title card

284. THE CURSE OF THE WEREWOLF, 1961

285 286 287 288 289 290 291 292

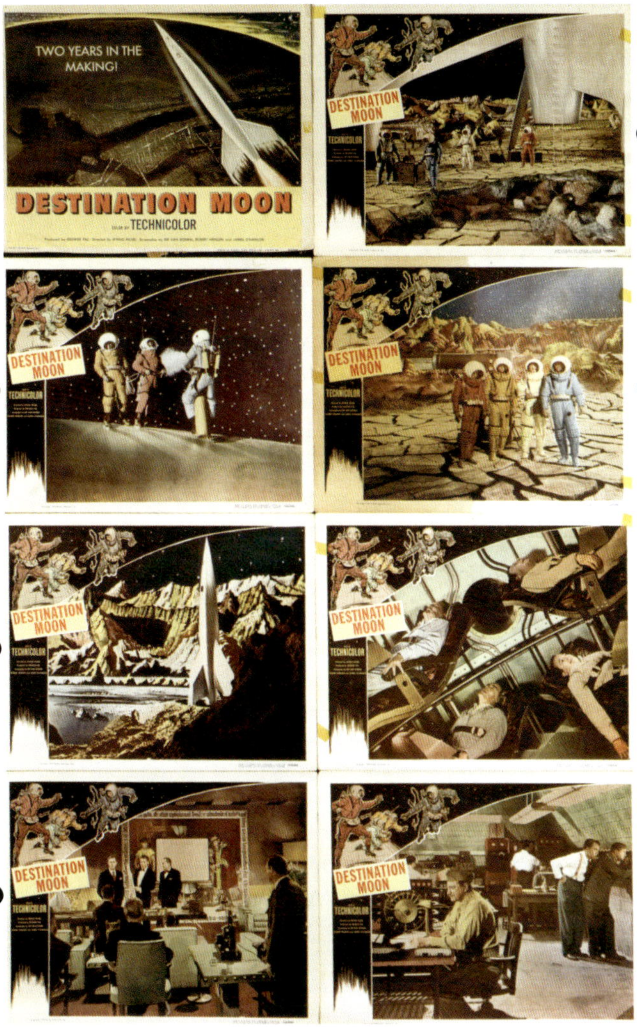

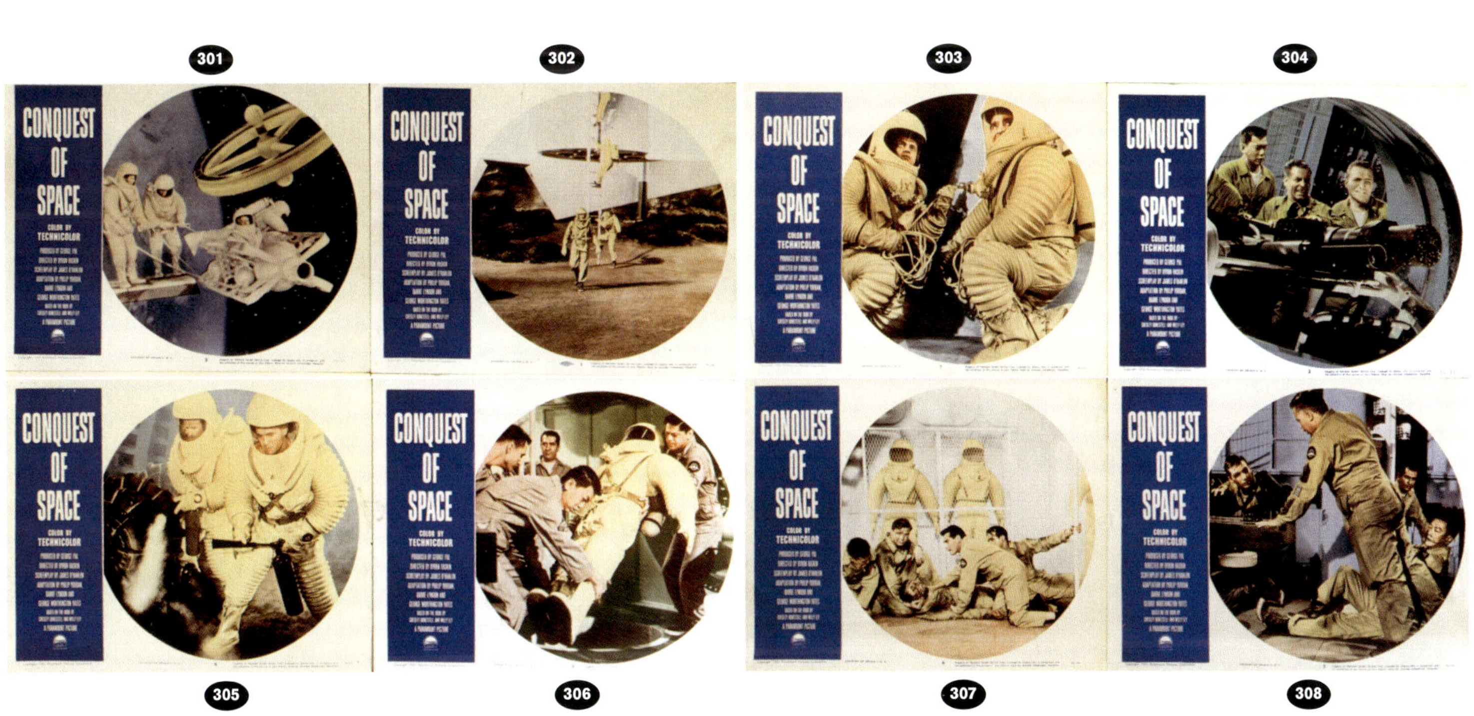

285-292. DESTINATION MOON, 1950

293 294 295 296 297 298 299 300

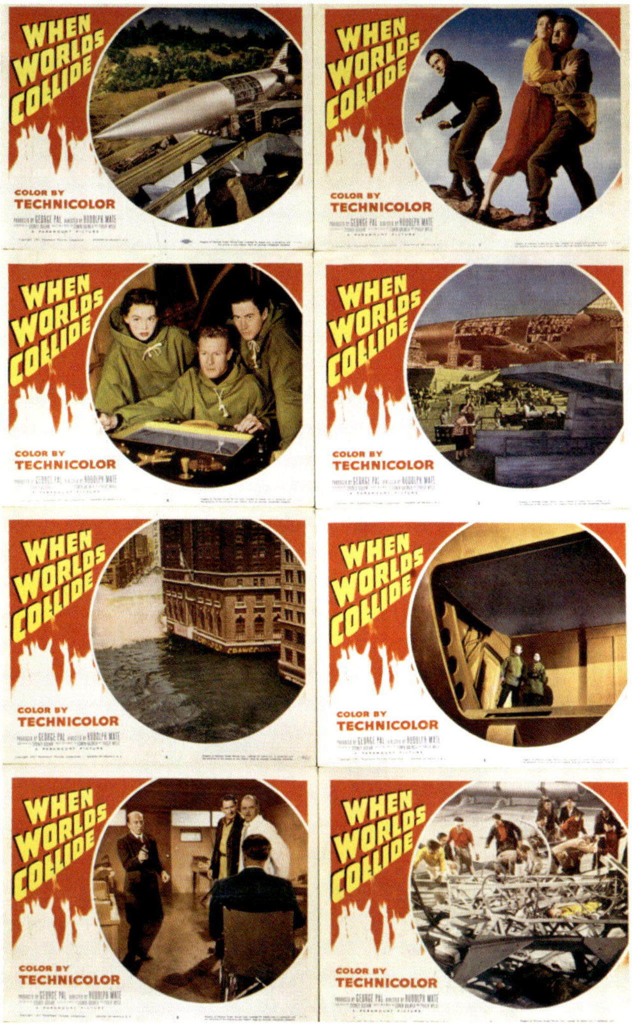

293-300. WHEN WORLDS COLLIDE, 1951

301 302 303 304

305 306 307 308

301-308. CONQUEST OF SPACE, 1955

309. THE WAR OF THE WORLDS, 1953, three-sheet

310. TARGET EARTH, 1954, three-sheet

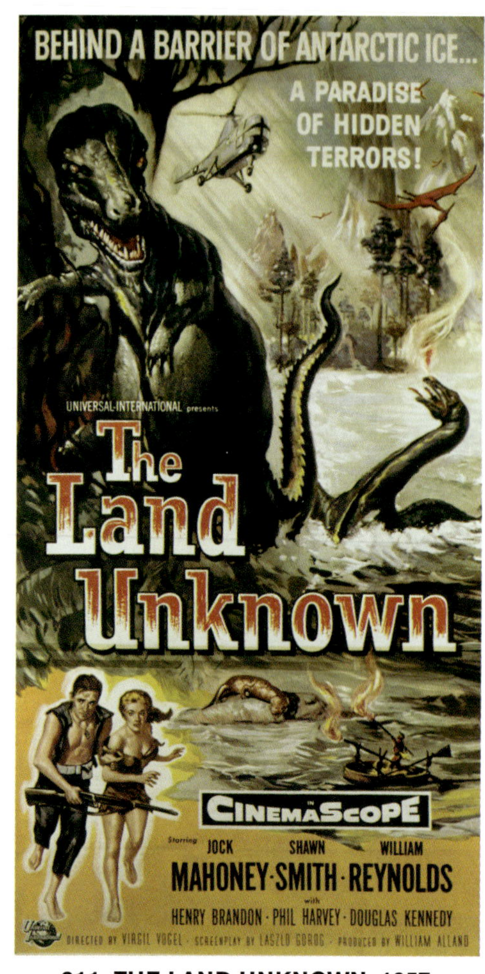

311. THE LAND UNKNOWN, 1957, three-sheet

312. THE MUMMY, 1959

313. BEAST FROM HAUNTED CAVE, 1959

314. I WAS A TEENAGE WEREWOLF, 1957

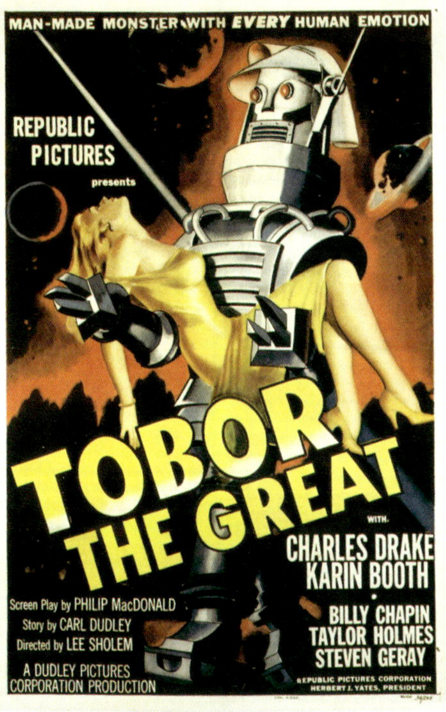

315. TOBOR THE GREAT, 1954

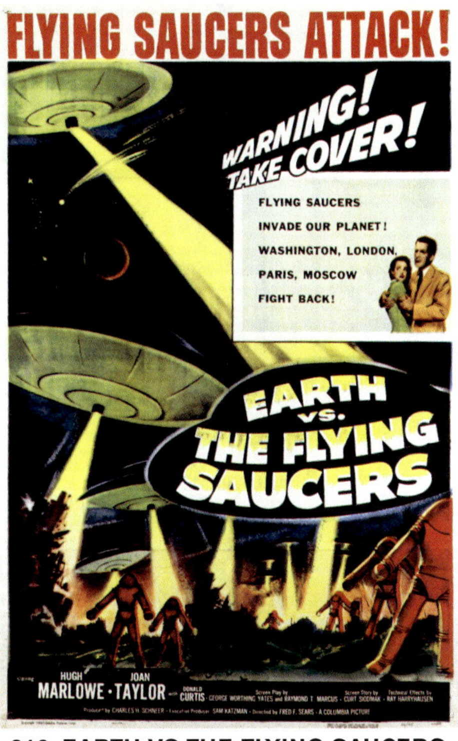

316. EARTH VS THE FLYING SAUCERS, 1956

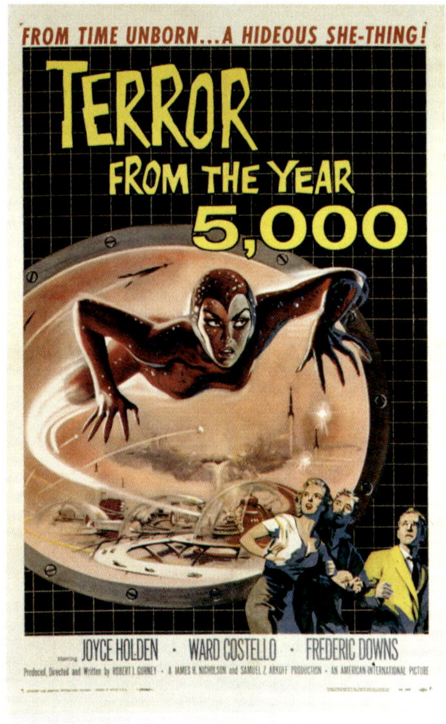

317. TERROR FROM THE YEAR 5,000, 1958

318

 319

320

 321

322

 323

324

 325

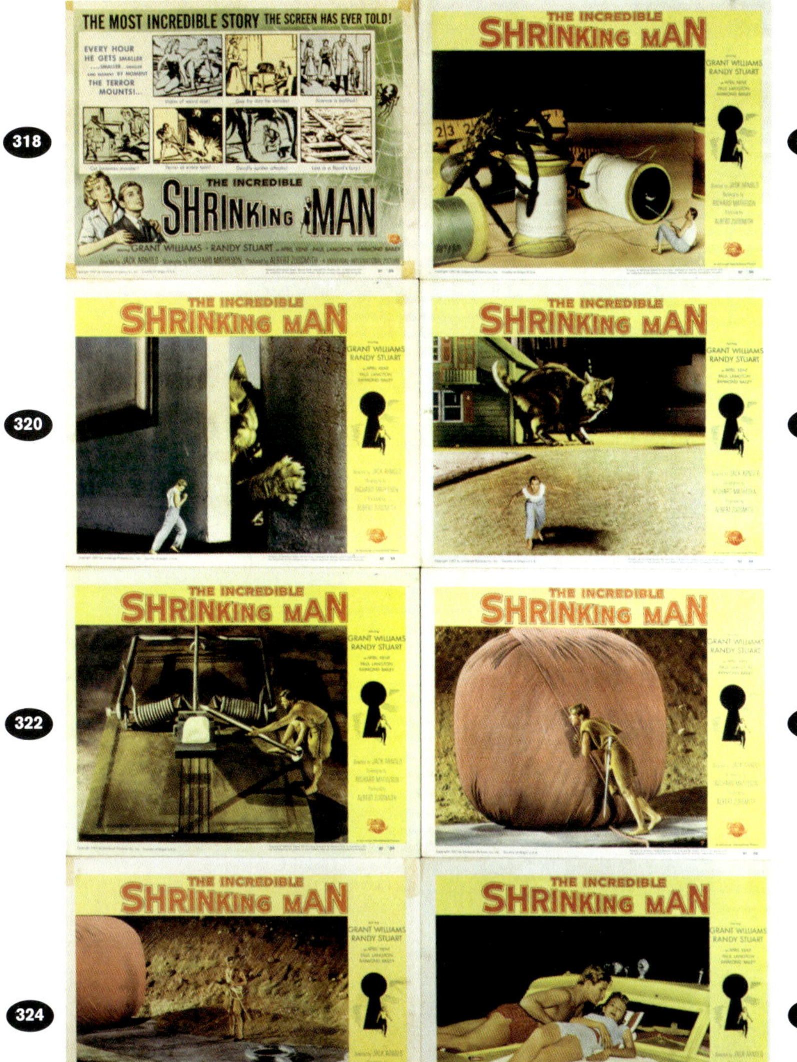

318-325. THE INCREDIBLE SHRINKING MAN, 1957, title card

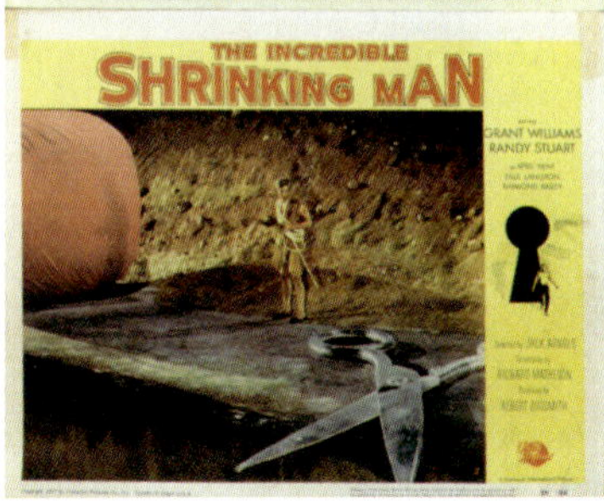

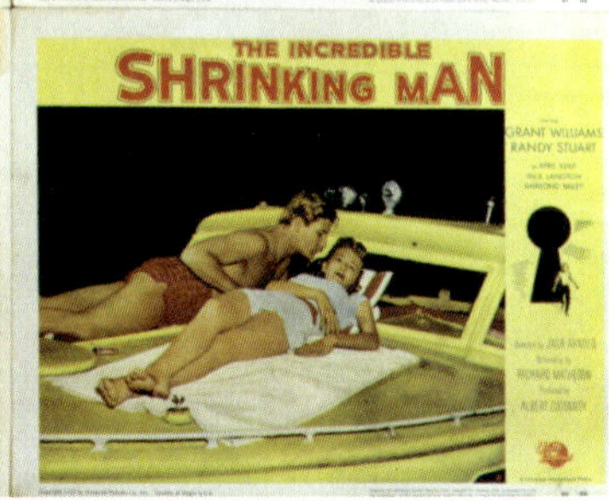

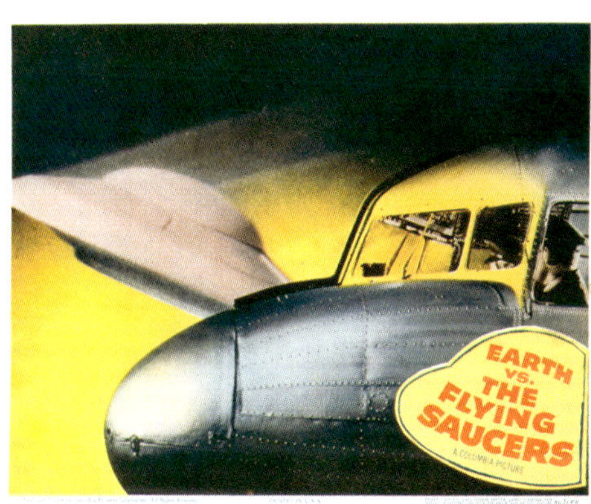

326. EARTH VS. THE FLYING SAUCERS, 1956

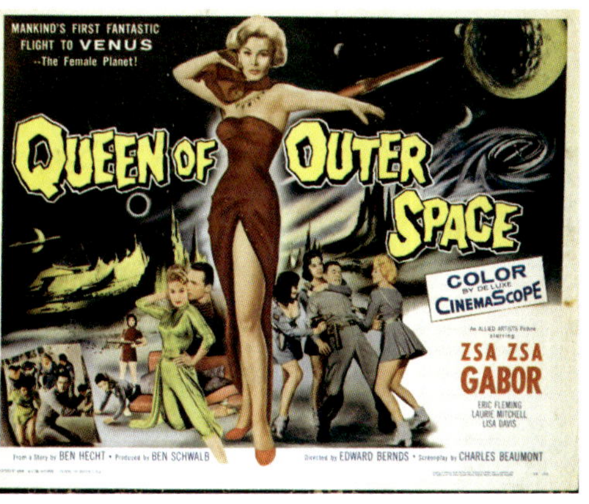

327. QUEEN OF OUTER SPACE, 1958, half-sheet

328. TARANTULA, 1955, half-sheet

329. TOBOR THE GREAT, 1954, half-sheet

330. THE WASP WOMAN, 1959

331. THE QUIET MAN, 1951, Japanese

332. EVERYTHING ENDS TONIGHT, 1954, Polish

333. WAGES OF FEAR, 1955, Russian

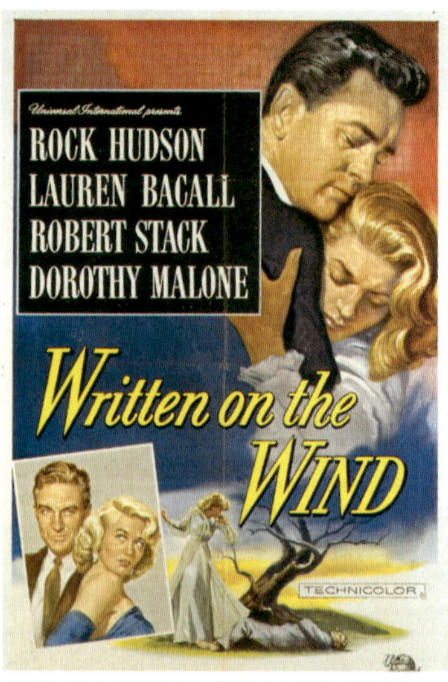

334. WRITTEN ON THE WIND, 1956

335. LOVE IN THE AFTERNOON, 1957

336. HIGH SCHOOL HELLCATS, 1958

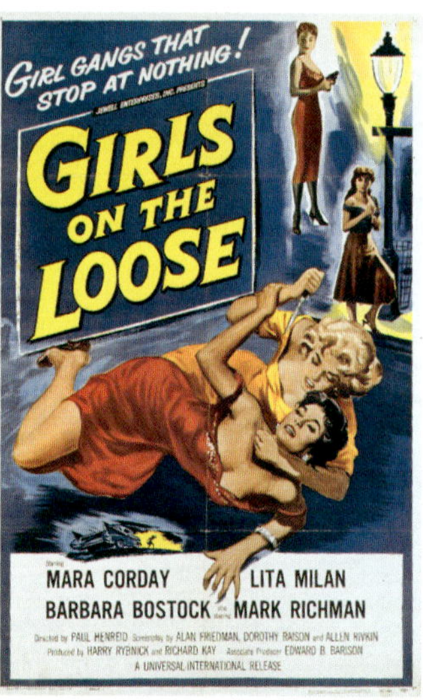

337. GIRLS ON THE LOOSE, 1958

338. HIDDEN FORTRESS, 1958, Japanese

339. PORGY & BESS, 1959, German

340. HIROSHIMA MON AMOUR, 1959, French one-panel

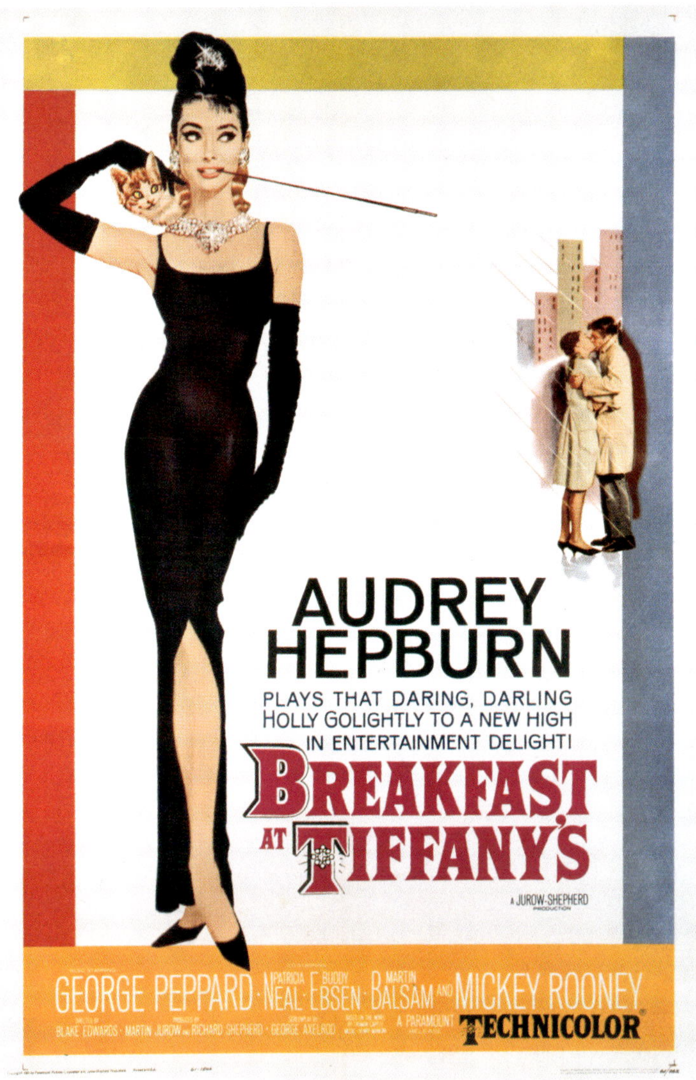

341. BREAKFAST AT TIFFANY'S, 1961

342. PSYCHO, 1960

343. THE HUSTLER, 1961

344. THE HUSTLER, 1961, Italian photobusta

345. PURPLE NOON, 1960, Argentinean

346. BLACK SUNDAY, 1961, French

347. JASON & THE ARGONAUTS, 1963, Italian one-panel

348. L'AVVENTURA, 1960, Japanese two panel

349. THE GREAT ESCAPE, 1963, three-sheet

350. LA DOLCE VITA, 1961, Spanish one-sheet

351. 8 1/2, 1983 re-release, Japanese

352. CLEOPATRA, 1964, British quad

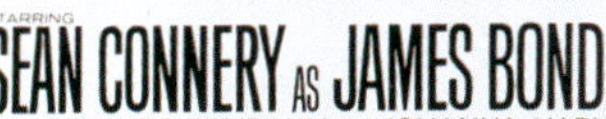
353. FROM RUSSIA WITH LOVE, 1964

354. GOLDFINGER, 1964, Japanese

355. A HARD DAY'S NIGHT, 1964

356. HELP, 1965

357. TO KILL A MOCKINGBIRD, 1963

358. FISTFUL OF DOLLARS, 1967, Italian

359. FOR A FEW DOLLARS MORE, 1967, German (rare style C)

360. DR STRANGELOVE, 1964

361. BEACH BLANKET BINGO, 1965, 30x40

362. THE SOUND OF MUSIC, 1966, Japanese

363. THE AMBUSHERS, 1967, set of 6 door panels

364. THE ENDLESS SUMMER, 1967 (very first release)

365. PUTNEY SWOPE, 1969

366. POINT BLANK, 1967, Polish

367. VALLEY OF THE DOLLS, 1967, Italian one-panel

368. 2001 A SPACE ODYSSEY, 1968, Japanese

369. TRASH, 1970

370. GET CARTER, 1971, Italian two-panel

371. THE OMEGA MAN, 1971, Italian one-panel

372. LE MANS, 1971, Italian two-panel

373. THE GETAWAY, 1972, Japanese

374. DISCREET CHARM OF THE BOURGEOISIE, 1972, Polish

375. THE GODFATHER, 1972

376. GODSON, 1972, French

377. SOLARIS, 1972, German

378. THE STING, 1974 (very rare style)

379. THE STING, 1974

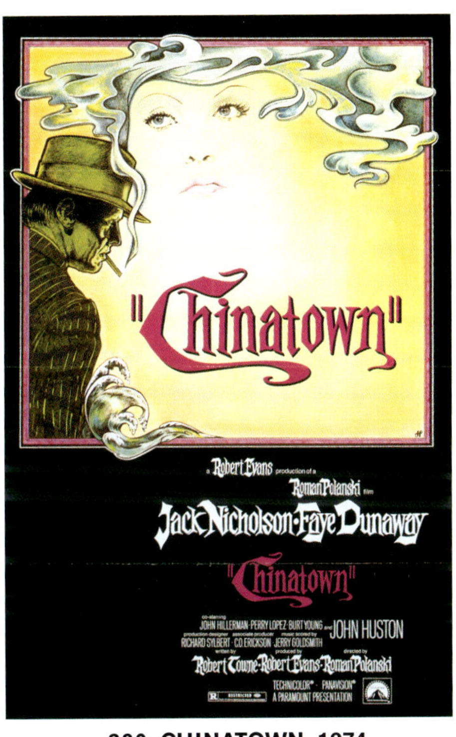

380. CHINATOWN, 1974

381. WHAT, 1973

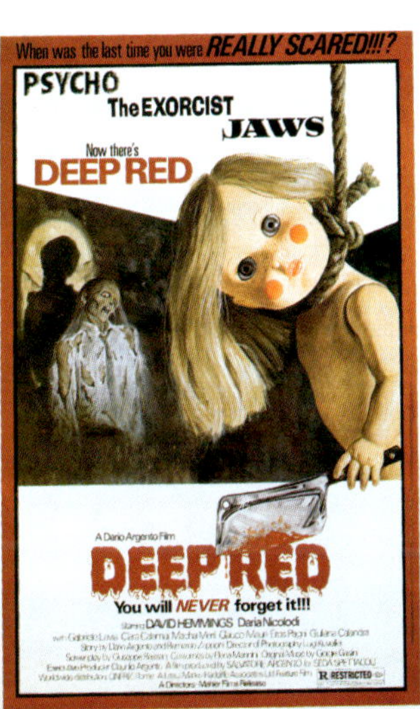

382. DEEP RED, 1975

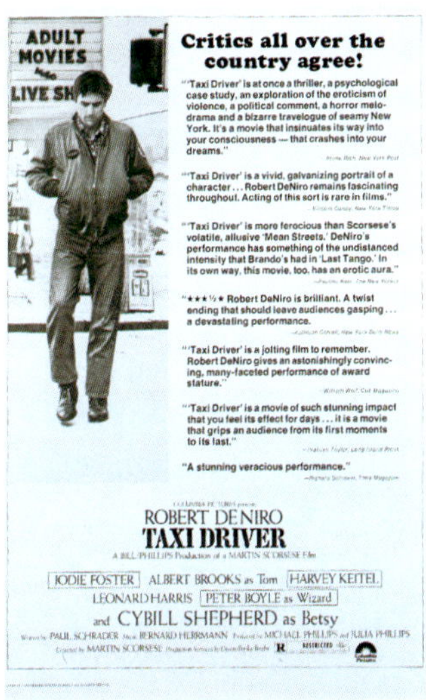

383. TAXI DRIVER, 1976

384. THE MAN WHO FELL TO EARTH, 1976, English one-sheet

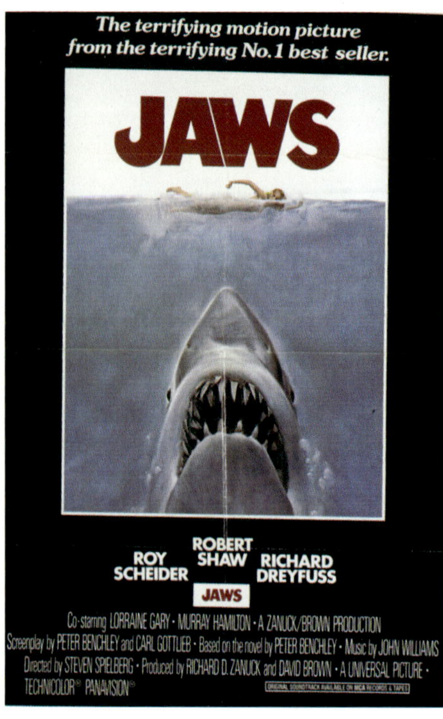

385. JAWS, 1975

386. THE KILLING OF A CHINESE BOOKIE, 1976

387. THE SHOOTIST, 1976, Italian one-panel

388. THE SHOOTIST, 1976

389. ROCKY, 1977

390. STAR WARS, 1977

391. SATURDAY NIGHT FEVER, 1977, 30x40

392. SATURDAY NIGHT FEVER, 1977

393. THE DEER HUNTER, 1978, English lobby card

394. HALLOWEEN, 1978

395. HALLOWEEN, 1978, Japanese

396. JAWS 2, 1978

397. UP IN SMOKE, 1978

398. GREASE, 1978

399. GREASE, 1978, 30x40

400. GREASE, 1978

401. THE LORD OF THE RINGS, 1978

402. ANIMAL HOUSE, 1978, subway poster

403. BABY SNAKES, 1979

404. APOCALYPSE NOW, 1979, 30x40

405. ALIEN, 1979, 30x40

406. QUADROPHENIA, 1979, French one-panel

407. THE BLUES BROTHERS, 1980

408. MAD MAX, 1980, English one-sheet

409. RAIDERS OF THE LOST ARK, 1981, 30x40

410. RAIDERS OF THE LOST ARK, 1981

411. SOMEWHERE IN TIME, 1980

412. SCARFACE, 1983

413. HELL'S ANGELS FOREVER, 1983

414. THE BREAKFAST CLUB, 1985

415. SID & NANCY, 1986

416. RAIN MAN, 1988

417. ET, 1982

418. THE LITTLE MERMAID, 1989

419. FRIDAY THE 13TH 8, 1989

420. FIELD OF DREAMS, 1989

421. PULP FICTION, 1994, Japanese

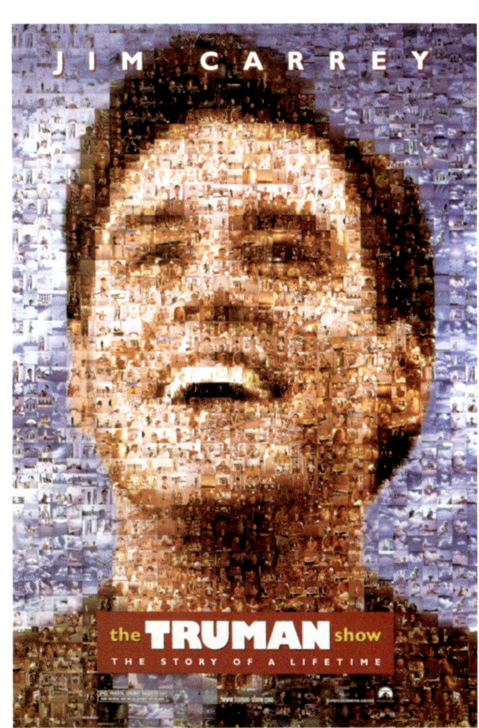

422. THE TRUMAN SHOW, 1998

423. AMERICAN BEAUTY, 1999

424. PHANTOM MENACE, 1999

Vintage Hollywood Posters VIII Index